Louisa May Alcott

Louisa May Alcott

AUTHOR OF *LITTLE WOMEN*

CHRISTIN DITCHFIELD

FRANKLIN WATTS
A Division of Scholastic Inc.
New York Toronto London Auckland Sydney
Mexico City New Delhi Hong Kong
Danbury, Connecticut

Photographs © 2005: Archive Photos/Getty Images/American Stock: 67; Boston Athenaeum: 44, 51 top; Corbis Images: 49, 55, 68, 75, 81, 93, 99 (Bettmann), 26 (Brooks Kraft), 16 (David Muench), 23, 62 (Lee Snider), 30, 90; Hulton | Archive/Getty Images/Stock Montage: 70; Library of Congress: cover (via SODA), 14, 36, 39; Orchard House/The Louisa May Alcott Memorial Association: cover background, back cover, 2, 6 left, 6 right, 9, 11, 37, 51 bottom, 63, 78, 83, 85, 87, 92, 95, 96; Stock Montage, Inc.: 66; Superstock, Inc.: 24 (Christie's Images), 40 (National Portrait Gallery, London, England); The Art Archive/Picture Desk/IUFM, Paris: 42; The Image Works/Topham: 71; Virginia Historical Society, Richmond, VA, Copyright 1996, Lora Robins Collection of Virginia Art: 82.

Library of Congress Cataloging-in-Publication Data

Ditchfield, Christin.
    Louisa May Alcott : author of Little women / by Christin Ditchfield.
        p. cm. — (Great life stories)
    Includes bibliographical references and index.
    ISBN 0-531-12403-7
    1. Alcott, Louisa May, 1832-1888—Juvenile literature. 2. Authors, American—19th century—Biography—Juvenile literature. I. Title. II. Series.
    PS1018.D58 2005

                                                                                            2004014314

Printed in the United States of America.
1 2 3 4 5 6 7 8 9 10 R 14 13 12 11 10 09 08 07 06 05

Contents

Louisa May Alcott's parents, called Bronson and Abba,
were very supportive of their children and encouraged their interests.

ONE

A Transcendental Family

On November 29, 1832, Amos Bronson and Abigail "Abba" May Alcott welcomed their second daughter into the world. Louisa May was named for her aunt, a woman with a soft voice and a gentle nature. As it turned out, little "Louy" was nothing like her namesake. Nor was she much like her older sister, Anna. Even as a toddler, Anna was prim and proper. She was a good little girl who behaved herself. Louisa had boundless energy, enthusiasm, and curiosity. She couldn't sit still. She wanted to explore everything in the world around her.

As a young girl, she loved to drive her hoop through the bustling streets of Boston and all the way down to the park at Frog Pond. During the 1800s, children often played with large wooden or metal barrel hoops. The object of the game was to keep the hoop rolling as fast and as far as possible. A short stick could be used to push the hoop along.

Once, Louisa chased her rolling hoop right into Frog Pond. She would never forget how a young African American boy jumped in and rescued her. Louisa liked to watch the jugglers and acrobats practicing for the circus on Beacon Street. Sometimes she could see the elephants on parade. Down at the harbor, she watched men unload ships full of boxes, barrels, and crates. Each package carried treasure, such as fruits, spices, and fabrics, from countries all over the world.

Sometimes Louy stopped to visit her Grandfather May. As they sat by the fire, he told her wonderful stories about the places he had been and the things he had seen and what life was like when he was a boy. Then he sent her home with little cakes, prunes, or other sweet treats. During the winter, Louy loved to slide down the snowy hill in the park and watch the rowdy boys go sledding. To little Louy, every day was a new adventure.

A LIFE OF LEARNING

Bronson and Abba were very unusual parents for that time. Back then, many people thought that "children should be seen and not heard." The Alcotts believed that children were unique individuals who should be encouraged to express their creativity. Bronson was not only a scholar and an educator, he was also a philosopher. He thought the best way to teach children was to listen to them. Let them share their ideas, he said. Then engage them in meaningful discussion. Bronson Alcott eagerly studied the development of his own children, documenting their growth in journals he later published.

The Alcott girls grew up in a home where life was all about learning. They didn't need to go to school to get an education. Every day began with a philosophical discussion over breakfast. Then the girls spent hours drawing, reading, writing, spelling, or studying mathematics. Lunch and dinner brought more opportunities for lively debate. Both father and teacher, Bronson taught each of his daughters how to read and write. He let them play around him as he worked in his study. He was writing hundreds of educational or scientific essays, articles, and books that he hoped to publish someday. Anna would sit quietly sewing, while Louisa built towers and bridges out of textbooks. From time to time, Bronson would stop his work to read to them—usually sermons or essays, favorite stories, or some of his own writings.

As loving and supportive as he could be, Bronson had to admit that he did not understand his second daughter at all. He was troubled by Louisa's spirited behavior, her willful and even stubborn personality, and her quick temper. Louisa had trouble sitting still. She never walked when she could run. If she was happy, she danced about the room wildly, shouting with glee. She

Louisa was an active, talkative child.

chattered incessantly. When it was too quiet, she had to stir things up, usually by teasing or pinching someone. Louisa could not have been more different from her gentle, soft-spoken, and easygoing father. Louisa knew that Bronson loved her. Yet all too often, she sensed his disappointment and disapproval. She wanted very much to please him, but she grew frustrated by what sometimes seemed like an impossible task.

SELF-IMPROVEMENT

The Alcotts were a part of the transcendentalist movement, which gained great popularity in the New England states during the mid-nineteenth century. Leaders of the movement included Ralph Waldo Emerson, Margaret Fuller, and Henry David Thoreau. Transcendentalists believed that intellectual and spiritual pursuits mattered more than material possessions. Character development was of the utmost importance. Self-sacrifice was often necessary. At all times, one should strive to be patient, kind, loving, generous, and unselfish.

This focus affected even the smallest events of family life. Louisa would always remember how it impacted her third birthday. The special occasion was to be celebrated with a party at her father's school. Louy was so excited that she could hardly control herself. Someone had baked a big plate full of delicious little cakes. Naturally, her mother and father insisted that the other students be served first. To the birthday girl, it seemed to take forever. At last, Louisa saw that there was just one more student in line. Then she noticed that there was only one cake left. Louisa quickly grabbed it for herself. Abba whispered to her, "It is always better to give away than to keep the nice things. I know my Louy will not let the little friend go without." Poor Louisa burst into tears as she handed over her special treat. She knew it was wrong to be selfish, but she did so want that "dear plummy cake."

The same year, Louisa's little sister Lizzie was born. Lizzie was sweet, gentle, and good-natured. Bronson absolutely doted on her. Now here was a girl after his own heart. Louisa adored Lizzie, too, but there were times when she felt pangs of jealousy. How could anyone be so perfect all the time?

As the girls grew older, Bronson would ask them to describe their greatest flaws or weaknesses. He expected his daughters to try to improve themselves. He encouraged them to record their attempts in a daily journal, as both he and Abba did.

THE TEMPLE SCHOOL

Bronson Alcott had opened his own school so he could teach children the way he believed they should be taught. For a time, the Temple School was quite successful. Bronson had as many as forty students, and

An illustration depicts the interior of the Temple School where Bronson taught his students through his own experimental methods.

their tuition paid his salary. It was just enough for the family to live on. Then in 1837, Bronson wrote a book about his experimental teaching methods. In many ways, it was simply a journal or record of what went on in the classroom on a daily basis. Bronson was not at all prepared for the response. While some philosophers found his theories fascinating, the parents of his students were alarmed. They did not know what to make of the controversial subjects he allowed their children to discuss. For example, when Bronson talked about the birth of an important historical figure, his students asked him where babies came from. In keeping with his philosophy, Bronson answered them. Of course, he explained human sexuality in such complicated and flowery language that very few of his students understood what he was talking about. He compared the physical relationship between a man and a woman to a kind of spiritual union that draws people closer to God. But in those days sex was a subject that was rarely mentioned at home, let alone at school. In a book he called *Conversations With Children on the Gospels*, Bronson appeared to encourage his students to question and dismiss some of the traditional doctrines of the Christian faith. At the same time, he compared himself and his revolutionary teachings to those of Jesus Christ. When these views became widely known, thirty students withdrew from the school.

Friends of the Alcotts had cautioned Bronson against releasing the book. They had warned him that he was going too far with some of his theories. People wouldn't understand them. But Bronson Alcott lived according to the dictates of his own conscience. He did what he thought was right. He never allowed public opinion to influence his actions. Now Bronson's educational philosophies were being attacked daily in newspaper editorials. From the pulpit, preachers publicly condemned his religious teachings. Bronson's supporters tried to defend him by explaining that his views were really not so extreme. Their best efforts could not overcome all the bad publicity he received.

For a few years, Bronson managed to keep the Temple School going with a handful of students. Then he accepted an African American student named Susan Robinson. Slavery was still legal at the time, although most northern states frowned on the practice. It would be more than a hundred years before society was ready to accept the idea of black and white students attending school together. All of Bronson's remaining students promptly withdrew. He was forced to close the school.

Louisa did not really understand what had happened, but she knew that her family was somehow in trouble. A dark cloud seemed to hang over the family home. The Alcotts faced a real struggle for survival. They had accumulated huge debts. Abba had to borrow money from her parents and siblings just to put food on the table. Bronson became deeply depressed. He sat alone in his study, with his head buried in his hands. More tragedy lay in store. On April 6, Abba gave birth to their long-awaited son, but sadly, he lived only a few short hours. In their heartache, the family drew strength and comfort from their love for one another.

A WELCOME INVITATION

Though his teaching methods may have raised questions, Bronson's transcendentalist philosophies attracted a lot of attention from other noted scholars. The Alcotts could count some of the most famous American authors, lecturers, and philosophers among their closest friends.

Despite the Temple School disaster, Ralph Waldo Emerson believed that Bronson Alcott had one of the finest minds of their era. He invited the Alcotts to move to Concord, Massachusetts. There they would find a whole community of people who shared their views. Bronson could give talks and discuss his philosophies with other great thinkers. Emerson said he would even arrange for the Alcotts to rent a cottage on a property near his own home. The Alcotts gratefully accepted his invitation.

Ralph Waldo Emerson

One of Bronson Alcott's closest friends was the world-famous author, poet, lecturer, and philosopher, Ralph Waldo Emerson. In 1836, Emerson set forth the basic principles of transcendentalism in his best-selling book, *Nature*. He taught that reality is something one discovers through meditation and spiritual reflection rather than through mere physical observation. For more than forty years, Emerson traveled the lecture circuit in the United States, Canada, and Great Britain. He gave as many as 1,500 speeches while continuing to write thought-provoking poems, essays, and books. Emerson inspired an entire generation of American authors, including Henry David Thoreau, Walt Whitman, Nathaniel Hawthorne, Margaret Fuller, and Louisa May Alcott.

By this time, the family had grown to include its youngest member, Abby May or "May." Louisa was hoping for a little brother, but she had to admit that her new little sister was very cute. Bronson, Abba, and their four daughters were ready to move to Concord to begin a new life.

It was a completely different atmosphere from that of the busy city. There were no tall buildings crowded together in city blocks, no factories, no shops, no traffic, no noise. Out in the country, there was plenty of sunshine and fresh air. There were wide open fields and forests with just a few farmhouses scattered in between. Still, it didn't take long for everyone to feel right at home. The Hosmer family lived next door. They had several children close in age to the Alcott girls. Anna was nine and quite grown up already. She had a crush on Henry Hosmer. Five-year-old Lizzie happily played dolls and hosted tea parties with Lydia Hosmer. And eight-year-old Louisa had finally found the little brother she always wanted. She and seven-year-old Cyrus Hosmer climbed trees, jumped fences, and raced each other around the barn. That summer, all of the children got together and decided to put on a series of plays. They dressed up in costumes and acted out their favorite fairy tales: "Cinderella" and "Jack and the Beanstalk." Anna might have been very prim and proper offstage, but onstage she suddenly became a dramatic actress. The boys played their roles with gusto. Lizzie and Lydia made up a cheerful and enthusiastic audience. And Louisa ran the entire show. She organized every production and assigned every part. She directed the other actors and often took a leading role herself.

When she wasn't playing with her sisters or the Hosmer children, Louisa spent all her time at the Emerson house. She loved their family as much as her own. Sometimes on her way to the Emersons, she would pass their new neighbor on the street. The great American novelist Nathaniel Hawthorne always greeted the child kindly.

In the fall, two young men opened a school very similar to the one Bronson had run in Boston. Henry David Thoreau and his brother John were members of the transcendentalist community and good friends of both the Emersons and the Alcotts. After years of getting lessons at home

One of Concord's most famous places is Walden Pond. Thoreau lived by this pond while he wrote one of his most popular books called *Walden.*

with their father, the Alcott children were thrilled to be able to attend this new school. Henry's classes nearly always consisted of outdoor field trips. He took his students through all the forests, swamps, and ponds in Concord. Thoreau showed the children where to find American Indian arrowheads and artifacts buried in the mud along the riverbanks. He taught them to identify countless flowers and trees and plants. He made moss and bark seem magical. Thoreau led his students to the best blueberries, huckleberries, and blackberries. He pointed out birds and squirrels and the tracks of other woodland animals. Louisa was in awe of her beloved teacher. His lessons fascinated her.

Henry David Thoreau

Louisa's favorite teacher would become one of America's most influential writers and thinkers. Henry David Thoreau first moved to Concord to be closer to his friend and mentor, Ralph Waldo Emerson. Thoreau desired freedom from the burden of material possessions. He wanted to live in harmony with nature. In 1845, Thoreau built a cabin on Walden Pond, where he spent his days observing nature in its tiniest detail. He wrote his thoughts and ideas in a journal that became his literary masterpiece, *Walden*.

Thoreau also wrote an essay called "Civil Disobedience." He said citizens should refuse to obey laws that violated their conscience. This kind of peaceful, nonviolent protest would be adopted by Mohandas Gandhi in India and the civil rights leader Martin Luther King, Jr. in the United States.

MONEY TROUBLES

The Alcotts loved their life in Concord, but the family's financial situation had not improved. Bronson thought he could make a living by giving lectures from his home. He thought people who appreciated his insights would offer to support him financially. They might pay him the same way they would pay someone who gave them music lessons or tutored them in their studies. But Bronson's lectures did not bring in the money he expected. It wasn't that people didn't enjoy listening to him talk. They came from miles around to sit in his living room and discuss transcendentalist philosophy. Unfortunately, Bronson never mentioned his desire for financial compensation, and it didn't occur to his guests to pay him for the time he spent with them. Bronson wrote a lot of articles and essays, but somehow his profound thoughts seemed to ramble on paper. His readers found them confusing. Once again, Bronson sank into depression. He couldn't support his family. They were on the verge of starvation, yet it didn't seem to occur to him that he might try some other method of earning a living. He thought of himself as an author, an educator, and a philosopher. He never once considered getting a "real" job. Abba was so worried and worn out from trying to make ends meet. Her relatives thought Bronson was practically insane. They pressured Abba to leave him and bring the girls back to Boston. Abba hated to keep asking for their help.

Ralph Waldo Emerson worried about his friend's inability to provide for his family. He recommended Alcott for speaking engagements and opened up opportunities for him to write for the transcendental magazine, *The Dial*. From time to time, Emerson gave the family financial support as well as much-needed encouragement. He gently offered advice that Bronson would have been wise to heed. Unfortunately, Bronson thought the suggestions would require him to compromise his principles. When the family's difficult situation turned into an all-out crisis, Emerson invited the Alcotts to move into his home with him and his family.

Before the Alcotts could decide what to do, Bronson was contacted by members of the transcendentalist movement in England. They had built several schools according to his model and had even named them after him. They would be honored if *the* Bronson Alcott would come to visit and lecture there. Alcott felt this opportunity could lead to even greater and more financially rewarding possibilities. So Emerson helped him raise the money to pay for his travel expenses. The girls bid their father a tearful farewell and waited eagerly for his return.

But when Bronson Alcott came back from England, they found that he had brought with him some strange new ideas that would bring even more challenges for the family.

Searching for
a Better Life

In England, Bronson Alcott met several men who shared his convictions. They longed to see the principles of transcendentalism put into practice. They envisioned a "New Eden," a paradise, where the distractions of the material world would not exist. In this paradise, intellectual and spiritual concerns would be the sole priority, the entire focus of everyday life. Bronson discussed the idea often with Charles Lane, his son William, and their friend Henry Wright. Eventually the men came to the conclusion that God wanted them to create such a place in the United States. This perfect community would serve as an example to the entire world. When Bronson returned home to Concord, he brought with him his new friends and their vision for "the garden of God" in New England.

FRUITLANDS

Louisa could hardly contain her joy at her father's homecoming celebration. The family had missed him so much. Louisa listened with interest as Bronson explained the great project they were about to undertake. It all sounded very grand and important. For several months the Lanes and Henry Wright shared the Alcotts' tiny home, as the men searched for suitable land and recruited volunteers to join them. Almost from the beginning, Charles Lane took over the household. He taught the girls their lessons. He controlled the conversation at the dinner table. Lane was much more strict than Bronson. He was more serious and aggressive in applying his principles to daily life. He frowned on whatever he perceived to be frivolousness. Lane even resented the affection that Bronson and Abba showed one another and their children. He thought it interfered with their ability to devote themselves fully to the cause. Bronson seemed willing to go along with whatever Lane decreed, but Abba disagreed with him. Louisa found that her joy about her father's homecoming quickly evaporated. The tension in the home dampened everyone's spirits.

To cheer her girls up, Abba decided to create a family "post office," a basket they could fill with little notes and treats for one another. At the end of each day, the "mail" would be delivered to the appropriate family members. It gave them something to look forward to during an otherwise difficult time.

In June of 1843, Charles Lane purchased a run-down property in the mountains to serve as the location of their new community. He and Bronson named the place Fruitlands. Though many people expressed interest in the project, few families were willing to give up everything they owned for an experiment. Even Wright had his doubts and decided to move to Boston. So in the end, it was the Alcotts, the Lanes, a Mr. Larned, a Mr. Palmer, and a Mr. Everett who set out to farm "God's acre." They would all live together as one "consociate family."

SUMMER IN PARADISE

It took a lot of hard work to make the dilapidated buildings at Fruitlands even liveable. The gardens and fields had to be planted so the "family" would have food. The Alcotts had always been vegetarians. Because of their poverty and their principles, they did not eat meat. Now the girls learned that no animal products were allowed—no milk, no eggs, no cheese. Meals consisted of apples, potatoes, and bread made without yeast (crackers).

The move to Fruitlands would be a difficult one for the Alcott family.

The people living at Fruitlands wanted to avoid wearing cotton clothing because slaves in the South were forced to harvest cotton crops.

There was only water to drink. Bronson and Charles Lane decided that to live in harmony with nature, people could not take anything from animals. In addition to dietary restrictions, this also meant no clothing made of leather or wool. Cotton was not acceptable because it was picked by slaves in the South. The family did not want to support or encourage slavery in any way. So Bronson and Lane designed uniforms that were made of linen, a fabric that comes from plant fibers.

A day at Fruitlands began at four or five o'clock in the morning. Only cold baths or showers were allowed. The girls still had daily lessons, which now included geometry and geography as well as grammar and spelling. They read, sewed, or wrote in their journals while the adults engaged in deep philosophical discussions and debates. Then there were chores to do. After lunch, the girls could play outdoors unsupervised. While they missed their friends from Concord, they loved to explore the fields and forests at the foot of the mountains.

Louisa wrote in her journal, "I ran in the wind and played . . . horse and had a lovely time in the woods with Anna and Lizzie. We were fairies, and made gowns and paper wings, I 'flied' highest of all."

In the evening, the family gathered around to sing, tell stories, and share with the visitors who had come to see how the experimental project was working. There were moments that summer when the community at Fruitlands seemed as wonderful as the family had hoped it could be. Unfortunately, those moments were few and far between.

NOT SO PERFECT AFTER ALL

By the time winter came, paradise had lost its charm. Abba and the girls carried the bulk of the workload. They were responsible for all of the household chores and most of the outdoor chores. They had to entertain a steady stream of guests. The men did not do their fair share. They were too busy writing about the experiment or going off on lecture tours to tell others about Fruitlands.

The "consociate family" emphasized extraordinary discipline as a means of achieving inner purity. Their lofty goals took their toll on Louisa. The fun-loving girl had too much spirit and not enough self-control. She knew she should be more obedient to her parents. She wanted to be kinder to her sisters. Between her father's disapproving looks and Lane's stern reprimands, Louisa ended up feeling "wicked" and miserable all the time. In her journal she wrote, "I was cross to-day, and I cried when I went to bed. I made good resolutions and felt better in my heart. If only I *kept* all I make, I should be the best girl in the world. But I don't, and so am very bad." For Louisa, it was a never-ending struggle. Years later, she

Louisa's Journals

All of her life Louisa May Alcott kept a diary or journal. She filled its pages with descriptions of her deepest thoughts and feelings, as well as notes on everyday events, and poems or bits of stories she was starting to write. As a child, Louisa shared her journals with her parents. They often made suggestions or offered words of encouragement. Louisa especially treasured the notes her mother wrote back. She found this one on her eleventh birthday:

"Your handwriting improves very fast. Take pains and do not be in a hurry. I like to have you make observations about our conversations and your own thoughts. It helps you to express them and to understand your little self. Remember, dear girl, that a diary should be an epitome of your life. May it be a record of pure thoughts and good actions, then you will indeed be the precious child of your loving mother."

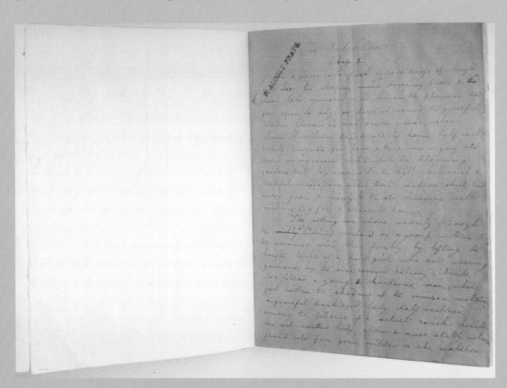

reread this passage in her diary and added a note to herself: "Poor little sinner! She says the same at fifty."

Lane's strict control over the family angered Abba. As the winter dragged on, Lane decided that no more firewood should be cut. Everyone should learn to live with the cold. If they forced themselves to endure it, their minds would grow stronger than their bodies. For Abba this was the last straw. Her children were now cold and sick as well as tired and hungry. Abba and Bronson argued constantly over Lane's increasingly harsh decrees. Fruitlands was tearing the Alcott family apart.

Abba made it clear that things could not continue this way. Bronson reluctantly agreed that he must put the well-being of his family above his philosophies and ideals. The Alcotts left Fruitlands in January of 1844.

A FRESH START

It was only half a house, a few rented rooms. But to Abba and the girls, their new home in Still River was heavenly. They were free to be their own little family again. The Alcotts still believed in the principles they had always lived by. They just didn't have to practice them under such difficult conditions. Abba inherited some money from her father's estate. It helped keep the family fed. Bronson wrote a series of essays on his sorrow over the failed Fruitlands experiment called "Sighs For Paradise." Yet even he was happier reflecting on the experience from a distance.

The Alcott girls had always studied at home or in small private schools with other children from families like their own. Now for the first time, the oldest girls attended a public school. There they met boys and girls from all over the neighborhood. Anna and Louisa learned that other families had values like their own. These families loved each other; their children tried to be good and do what was right. However, unlike the transcendentalists, these families did not see physical comfort and material possessions as obstacles to spiritual growth. When the parents of their classmates heard about the Alcotts' restricted diet, they worried that the girls weren't getting enough nutrition. Soon, these parents began sending extra food in their children's lunches, to be shared with the Alcott sisters. Anna and Louisa tasted all kinds of new treats: pickles, bananas, doughnuts!

Their cheerful young teacher, Miss Maria Chase, was nothing like the stern Charles Lane. She did not appear to be overly concerned about her students' progress in their studies. Whenever she could, she took them out of the classroom to go on hayrides and picnics. At thirteen, Anna quickly made friends with the other "young ladies" in the class. Twelve-year-old Louisa still preferred the company of boys. At recess, she demonstrated that she could climb as high, run as fast, and throw a ball as far as any of them.

BACK TO CONCORD

Over the years, the Alcott family rarely stayed in one place for any length of time. Often, it was a necessity. When they could no longer afford one home, they moved to another. Sometimes they moved in hope of improving their situation. They thought they might have more opportunities for a better life somewhere else.

While they were at Fruitlands, the Alcotts had distanced themselves from the Emersons. Lane disapproved of the Emerson family. He said that for people who claimed to reject the material world, they lived very comfortably. Although Emerson would not openly criticize Lane, he believed that Lane's views were too extreme. Emerson hoped that Bronson would eventually come to his senses. Fruitlands had failed, and Bronson was free of Lane's influence. Emerson sought to restore their friendship. He offered to purchase a few acres of land for the family back in Concord. Until they had found a suitable home, they could stay with their old friends, the Hosmers. The Alcotts would be reunited with the more moderate members of the transcendentalist community. They could challenge, encourage, and inspire one another. They could share their ideas and engage in lively debate once again. The Alcotts were thrilled to accept Emerson's offer. It was a joyous reunion on all sides.

With Emerson's help, the family purchased an old house they called Hillside. For several months, Bronson and John Hosmer worked diligently to renovate the home. They repaired the porch, the stairs, and the roof. They added bedrooms and bathrooms. Bronson took particular interest in the gardens and orchards. He discovered that he enjoyed working with his hands. Abba made the house a home. As she went about putting things in order, she often sang with joy. All four girls eagerly helped with chores—sewing, cooking, cleaning, and fetching wood for the stove. Ever a tomboy, Louisa joined her father in pulling weeds and planting seeds. Anna would sit nearby, reading or sewing. Lizzie had such a sweet, gentle nature. For the most part, she was content just to watch the others at work or play. Abby May was another story. She loved to be the center of attention, prancing all over the place.

Sometimes the Alcotts went on family outings. They took long walks through the forests and fields of Concord. They visited Henry

Pilgrim's Progress

For as long as she could remember, *Pilgrim's Progress* had been Louisa's favorite book. It was written by John Bunyan in 1678. The book tells the story of a man named Christian who leaves his home in the City of Destruction to begin a perilous journey. Christian overcomes many trials and temptations along the way, arriving at last at the Celestial City. As a pastor, Bunyan wrote this allegory to speak to those who suffer hardships and learn important lessons on their own spiritual journey. All of the Alcotts could relate to this theme. Throughout her life, Louisa often referred to the story, comparing her experiences to scenes from the book. Bunyan's story taught her courage and perseverance. It gave her comfort and encouragement.

Millions of others have felt as Louisa did. Since its publication, *Pilgrim's Progress* has sold more copies and has been translated into more languages than any other book beside the Bible. More than three hundred years after it was written, it remains a best-seller.

THE
Pilgrim's Progress.
FROM
THIS WORLD
TO
That which is to come.
The Second Part.
Delivered under the Similitude of a
DREAM,
Wherein is set forth
The manner of the setting out of Christian's Wife and Children, their
Dangerous JOURNEY,
AND
Safe Arrival at the Desired Country.

By JOHN BUNYAN,

I have used Similitudes, Hos. 12. 10.

LONDON,
Printed for Nathaniel Ponder at the Peacock, in the Poultry, near the Church, 1684.

David Thoreau on Walden Pond. He took his former students for a ride in his boat. Mr. Hosmer opened his own private school, which all of the Alcott girls attended. After lessons, the sisters gathered their friends and neighbors to help them put on their favorite plays. They acted out their own versions of classic stories such as *Oliver Twist* and *Pilgrim's Progress*. Now that they were older, the children could add more in the way of costumes and sets. They could deliver longer speeches; there were more speaking parts. As always, Louisa was the director and lead actor. She wrote all of the scripts herself.

Life seemed much better in every way. Louisa couldn't understand why she suddenly felt moody and restless all the time.

THREE

Discovering Her Dream

Louisa had a passionate personality. She felt every emotion deeply. These feelings only grew stronger as the tomboy became a teenager. Louisa had been raised to question and consider everything she experienced and to form her own opinions. She began to understand why her family struggled so much. While she loved him dearly, Louisa could see her father's faults and failures. It frustrated her to realize just how difficult life had been for her long-suffering mother. Louisa also became aware of how different she was from other girls. She had never cared for dolls and tea parties. She had always been active and adventurous. She wanted to be doing something meaningful with her life. But what?

With all these thoughts and emotions tumbling around in her head, Louisa desperately needed time to be alone. She longed to be able to think her way through things and sort them out. She wished she could have a room of her own, a place where she could go and shut the door. It just didn't seem possible. Instead, Louisa went for long walks in the countryside. Surrounded by nature, she found a peace and quiet that refreshed her. Her spirits were lifted, at least for a while. In her journal, she wrote of one particularly memorable experience:

> I had an early run in the woods before the dew was off the grass. The moss was like velvet, and as I ran under the arches of yellow and red leaves I sang for joy, my heart was so bright and the world so beautiful. I stopped at the end of the walk and saw the sunshine out over the 'Virginia meadows.'
>
> It seemed like going through a dark life or a grave into heaven beyond. A very strange and solemn feeling came over me as I stood there, with no sound but the rustle of the pines, no one near me, and the sun so glorious, as for me alone. It seemed as if I *felt* God as I never did before, and I prayed in my heart that I might keep that happy sense of nearness in my life.

"THE POET'S CORNER"

As they renovated Hillside, Bronson and Abba decided to grant Louisa's wish and give her a room all to herself. Louisa could hardly believe it. In March of 1846, she wrote, "I have at last got the little room I have wanted so long and am very happy about it. It does me good to be alone, and Mother has made it very pretty and neat for me. My work-basket and desk are by the window, and my closet is full of dried herbs that smell very nice. The door that opens into the garden will be very pretty in summer, and I can run off to the woods when I like."

Then she added, "I have made a plan for my life, as I am in my teens, and no more a child. I am old for my age, and don't care much for girl's things. People think I'm wild and queer, but Mother understands and helps me. I have not told any one about my plan, but I'm going to *be* good. I've made so many resolutions, and written sad notes, and cried over my sins, and it doesn't [sic] seem to do any good! Now I'm going to *work really*, for I feel a true desire to improve, and be a help and comfort, not a care and sorrow, to my dear mother."

The Alcotts referred to Louisa's room as "the poet's corner." Indeed, Louisa now spent all of her free time at her desk, pouring out her emotions as poetry. Years earlier, when Louisa had written her first poem, Abba had proudly exclaimed, "You will grow up a Shakespeare!" For her fourteenth birthday, Louisa received a new pen as a birthday gift from her mother. Abba included a few lines from a poem by John Greenleaf Whittier:

> *Oh may this pen your muse inspire,*
> *When wrapt in pure poetic fire,*
> *To write some sweet, some thrilling verse . . .*

Louisa was filled with awe at the thought of having her words inspire people the way others' words inspired her. Of course, Louisa already had loyal fans. Anna, Lizzie, and Abby May loved to visit "the

poet's corner" and listen to Louisa read her
latest poem or the script she was writing for
their next production. Louisa had begun to
create her own full-length plays, each with as
many as fourteen scenes. She let her imagination run wild as she wrote epic stories of
star-crossed lovers in faraway lands, daggers
and spells, heroes and villains, and damsels in
distress. These plays had titles like "The
Witch's Curse," "The Mysterious Page," and
"The Captive of Castile." The girls couldn't
wait to act them out onstage.

Though she was growing into a young
woman, Louisa didn't mind playing all the
male roles. She would much rather cross
swords with an evil count or climb a tower
to save a princess than faint, swoon, or burst
into tears as the heroines usually did. Still, the
women in Louisa's plays were much more
powerful and crucial to the plot than the
female characters in other dramas of the
time. Anna, Lizzie, and Abby May played
these parts with great enthusiasm. The sisters
formed a club based on one of their favorite
novels, *The Pickwick Papers* by Charles Dickens.
They each took the name of one of Dickens's
characters: Pickwick, Tupman, Winkle, and

Snodgrass. The "gentlemen" published their own newspaper, with each one contributing a story, poem, or announcement of some kind. Louisa served as editor-in-chief. As she churned out page after page, Louisa knew she had found her lifelong love. Somehow she was meant to be a writer.

Louisa and her sisters created their own newspaper. A page from one of the issues is shown here.

A DEAR FRIEND

Bronson had not been able to find work since the family moved to Concord. Several times he had applied to teach at one of the district schools. He was now willing to consider modifying his methods and employing a more traditional approach to teaching. But his neighbors remembered the Fruitlands disaster. They had heard all kinds of rumors about what went on there. They repeatedly refused Bronson's applications. Bronson kept himself busy working in his garden or studying for hours on end, but these activities didn't pay anything. In the summer of

Open Hearts, Open Home

The Alcott family always struggled to make ends meet, but their own poverty did not keep them from reaching out to those less fortunate. They welcomed needy people into their home, even when they barely had enough food to feed themselves. Their visitors stayed for weeks, months, sometimes years. Long-term guests included an orphaned boy and a mentally disabled teenage girl.

Not everyone who enjoyed the Alcotts' hospitality was in dire circumstances. Scholars and lecturers and philosophers were frequent guests at the Alcott home. For four months, the Alcotts even made room for Charles Lane, the man who had been so difficult to live with at Fruitlands, when he came to visit them at Hillside. For the Alcott family, courtesy and kindness were the rule. Bronson and Abba believed that material possessions were to be shared, not hoarded. They had received the generosity of others, and they gave freely themselves.

1848, both Bronson and Abba were invited to take over the management of a sanitarium, a kind of health spa, in Maine. Abba thought it was a great offer. The double salary would be a big help. After all, they had mouths to feed. Bronson wouldn't even consider it. He had no interest in supervising invalids at a recovery hospital. Abba shocked the family by announcing that she would go herself, at least for the summer. She took Abby May with her. Following her mother's lead, Anna accepted a job teaching summer school in New Hampshire. It would bring in a little money. The family had relatives there she could stay with.

Without her mother and two of her sisters, Louisa found Hillside a rather dull place to spend the summer. Father continued to work in his garden or his study. Lizzie was still at home. The two sisters had grown very close. Lizzie so admired Louisa's adventurous spirit, while Louisa

To help the family, Abba went to work at a sanitarium in Maine.

thought Lizzie was as dear and gentle and sweet as any human being could be. Each one wished to be more like the other. But although the girls enjoyed spending time together, Lizzie could be just as content playing by herself with her dolls.

Nearly every day, Louisa walked over to the Emerson house in search of company and conversation. Mr. Emerson had been such a good friend to the Alcotts. Now that she was old enough to carry on an adult conversation, Louisa found that he was also a very good listener. He asked her questions and encouraged her to share her thoughts with him. It amazed Louisa that a brilliant and accomplished man like Mr. Emerson would treat her with such respect. A successful author himself, Emerson took an interest in Louisa's writing. He taught her things he had learned. He introduced her to books by other authors, such as Wordsworth, Coleridge, Dante, Goethe, Plato, Shakespeare, that he knew would inspire her. They were all so wonderful, they made Louisa's head spin. Emerson gave her permission to borrow books from his extensive library any time she liked. She loved to hear him read aloud to his own children. Unlike her father, Emerson never made Louisa feel that she was a disappointment to him or that he disapproved of her somehow. She revered Emerson as a hero.

Emerson introduced Louisa to the work of great writers, such as William Shakespeare.

As the days and weeks went by, Louisa decided to turn the Hillside barn into a schoolroom. She would teach the Emerson children as a way to repay Mr. Emerson for his many kindnesses. Louisa gave them lessons in language, math, science, and geography. Little Ellen Emerson was her favorite. Ellen loved to hear Louisa tell stories, and her enthusiasm inspired Louisa's creativity. Louisa made up dozens of stories for Ellen about elves, fairies, and their woodland adventures. Later, she wrote them all down for her in a little book she titled *Flower Fables*. Louisa's young pupil absolutely adored her.

ANOTHER MOVE

Abba hated being away from her husband and daughters, but money had to be earned somehow. Working at the sanitarium in Maine, Abba became convinced that her family would be better off living in a big city. Bronson could give lectures again at universities, clubs, and philosophical societies. Anna and Louisa were both old enough to teach. Abba could look for a situation similar to the one she had in Maine, a job that would employ her considerable organizational and management skills. Abba's relatives begged her to come to Boston. They wanted to help the family. They knew of a position that would be perfect for Abba. She could operate their mission to the city's poor and needy.

In November of 1848, the Alcotts held a family council to discuss the possibility of moving to Boston. None of them wanted to leave Hillside and their friends in Concord. But as Bronson thought about it, he began to get excited about sharing his philosophies with a new audience. He would not be too sorry to leave a community that did not

A Woman's Work

In the 1800s, there were not many jobs open to women. Most women married young and devoted themselves to raising families. Married women almost never worked outside the home. Single women lived with relatives. They took care of the family's young children or helped with household chores. A woman might become a teacher, a seamstress, a housekeeper, a nurse, or companion. There were few other options.

Early on, Abba Alcott had insisted, "My girls shall have trades." She taught them every skill she could think of that might help them earn their own living someday. Abba did not want her daughters to be completely helpless and totally dependent on their husbands or relatives. If they ever found themselves alone—unmarried, widowed, or with a husband perpetually out of work—they would at least be able to do something to help support themselves and their families.

respect him or his ideas. The girls were willing to work and were even anxious to find ways to help the family. The more they talked about it, the better moving to Boston sounded. At last the decision was made. The Alcotts would move to the city. As Louisa listened to the family discussion, she made a silent decision of her own. She was tired of being poor. She was tired of having to make do, tired of moving from place to place when the money ran out. Somehow she would find a way to support her family. One day their struggles would be nothing more than a memory. She would sew, teach, act, or write, whatever it took. Louisa was determined to be "rich and famous and happy" before she died.

The Alcotts returned to Boston in 1848, hoping to find better work opportunities.

A Published Author

It had been almost ten years since the Alcotts last lived in Boston. When they returned in the fall of 1848, they found a very different city. A wave of immigrants had crossed the ocean in search of a better life. They came from Ireland, Italy, Israel, Syria, and China. More than fifty thousand of them settled in Boston. Unfortunately these new Americans had a hard time adjusting to their adopted country. Very few spoke English, and even fewer could read or write. They did not have the skills or training they needed to find work. They lived in slums—filthy, run-down neighborhoods riddled with crime, poverty, and disease. Many were on the verge of starvation. The Alcotts had faced their share of hardships. The family understood the struggle to make ends meet. But these people were the poorest of the poor. They desperately needed assistance.

A group of Boston's wealthiest citizens, including some of Abba's relatives, got together to discuss the crisis facing the city and what could be done about it. These community leaders were willing to donate a tremendous amount of money to the cause, but they wanted to be sure their money would be well spent. Someone should evaluate the situation and determine the greatest areas of need. Someone should report to the committee with specific information about potential projects and the proposed costs. Someone should then create programs that offered education and job training, and then organize the distribution of food, clothing, and medicine.

The committee decided that "someone" was Abba Alcott. No one was more compassionate—or capable. She would be paid a small monthly salary to coordinate the citywide outreach.

SHARING RESPONSIBILITIES

Abba threw herself wholeheartedly into this new mission. She worked day and night to rescue the downtrodden. As a result she was hardly ever home. Bronson once again found an eager audience for his philosophical lectures. He attracted a following, a small group of intellectuals and academics who met regularly to listen to him. Bronson also began working on a book that he thought would be his life's work. When he wasn't lecturing, he was locked in his study writing feverishly. Anna took a job as a live-in nanny, or governess, at the home of a nearby family. Her salary went toward the family's expenses. Lizzie and May were still in school, and so it fell to Louisa to keep the home in order. Cooking and cleaning had never been Louisa's favorite activities. She found housework dull and tiresome. She did want to contribute to the family, but she felt that somehow there was more she could be doing. In her diary, she poured out her frustrations:

> So long a time has passed since I kept a journal that I hardly know how to begin. Since coming to the city, I don't seem to have thought much, for the bustle and dirt and change send all lovely images and restful feelings away. . . . Seventeen years I have lived, and yet so little do I know, and so much remains to be done before I begin to be what I desire—a truly good and useful woman.
>
> In looking over our journals, Father says, 'Anna's is about other people, Louisa's about herself.' That is true, for I don't *talk* about myself; yet must always think of the willful, moody girl I try to manage, and in my journal I write of her to see how she gets on. Anna is so good she need not take care of herself, and can enjoy other people. If I look in my glass, I try to keep down vanity about my long hair, my well-shaped head, and my good nose. In the street I try not to covet fine things. My quick tongue is always getting me into trouble, and my moodiness makes it hard to be cheerful when I think how poor we are, how much worry it is to live, and how many things I long to do I never can. So every day is a battle . . .

Not long after they arrived in Boston, the entire Alcott family came down with smallpox. The girls got over the infection quickly, but Bronson nearly died. It took a long time and a lot of rest for him to recover his strength. Through it all, Louisa kept the household running.

She nursed her parents back to health. She wrote skits and stories to amuse everyone and keep their spirits up.

A WELCOME CHANGE

Eventually, Lizzie decided to drop out of school. She was shy and hated being out among strangers. She had no scholarly ambition. Lizzie only wanted to be home with her family. Bronson and Abba were disappointed with their daughter's decision, but Louisa welcomed the news. Lizzie gladly took over the housekeeping duties. It gave her joy to watch over the family and make their little house a home. Louisa was free to look for other work.

Over the next several years, Louisa found many different ways to earn money. Sometimes she worked as a teacher, tutor, or governess, like Anna. One year, the two sisters opened their own school together. They taught a small group of students in their home. In those days, anyone could start a school. To be a teacher, a person only needed to know more than his or her students. There were no laws governing the state of education. Attendance was not mandatory. Most poor children didn't go to school at all. Some children were taught at home by their parents or by paid tutors. Some attended community schools, private schools, or one of a handful of public schools. With the rigorous education they had received from their own parents, Anna and Louisa were far more qualified than most teachers of their day.

Later on, Louisa accepted a position as a companion to a woman whose illness confined her to bed. When Louisa arrived at the woman's home, she learned that she was actually expected to work as a servant.

From sunup to sundown, Louisa washed dishes, scrubbed floors, shoveled snow, and chopped wood. When her patient's brother kept trying to force his affections on her, Louisa decided she had had enough. She walked out. For seven weeks' work, she had been paid only four dollars. She should have received three or four times as much!

Fighting for Their Rights

In 1848, the first women's rights convention was held in Seneca Falls, New York. Elizabeth Cady Stanton and Lucretia Mott organized the event. They wanted to draw attention to the way women had been denied their most basic civil rights, and the inequality with which they were treated by the laws of the land. Abba Alcott quickly joined the movement in Boston. She petitioned the state of Massachusetts to grant woman suffrage, or the right to vote. It would take another seventy years and a constitutional amendment to bring about this change. Many women fought the battle, and Louisa May Alcott was among them. Ever her mother's daughter, she actively campaigned for women's rights throughout her lifetime.

In between and in addition to teaching positions, Louisa took on all kinds of odd jobs. She made two dollars a week doing laundry and sewing. It was a fair wage at the time. Louisa discovered that sewing suited her best. Hemming pillowcases did not take a lot of energy or concentration. While her fingers flew, her mind was free to plot out new stories. These stories had always entertained her family and friends. Soon, Louisa's writing would help her support them.

A WORKING WRITER

Louisa had known for some time that she was meant to be a writer. Ideas were constantly churning in her head. She had such a rich imagination. Sometimes Louisa had stayed up all night putting her stories down on paper. Now she began to dream about the possibility of getting her work published. Using the pen name Flora Fairfield, nineteen-year-old Louisa submitted one of her poems to *Peterson's Magazine*. It printed "Sunlight" in 1851. Louisa began sending out some of the stories she had written years before. *The Olive Branch* printed "The Rival Painters" and paid her five dollars for it. *Dodge's Literary Museum* accepted another story entitled "A Masked Marriage." For this one, Louisa received ten dollars. As time went on, Louisa decided to take a professional approach to writing. She studied popular magazines to see what types of stories they published and what style they liked. Then she wrote stories specifically for these magazines.

One of her stories was rejected by a publisher named James T. Fields. He told Louisa that she should stick to teaching. "You cannot write," he said. Louisa refused to be discouraged by his harsh pronouncement. She took his words as a personal challenge. She *could* write, and she did. Her work continued to be published, often under a variety of pen names. It was a popular practice in those days to disguise one's identity and create a fictitious persona—an imaginary "author." It added a sense of mystery and intrigue for the reader. And it gave the real author the opportunity to write freely about subjects they might not have felt comfortable addressing under their own names.

Several of Louisa's stories appeared in the prestigious *Saturday Evening Gazette*. She wrote book reviews for a newspaper. One of her plays was performed by a local theater group. Later, a publisher expressed interest in the collection of fairy tales that Louisa had written for Ellen Emerson. In December of 1854, these stories were published as *Flower Fables*, Louisa's very first book. She presented a copy to her mother with the following note:

Dear Mother,

Into your Christmas stocking I have put my 'first-born,' knowing that you will accept it with all its faults. . . . Whatever beauty or poetry is to be

James T. Fields told Louisa that she was a terrible writer, but she didn't let his criticism stop her from writing her stories.

Flower Fables was Louisa's first published book.

FLOWER FABLES

LOUISA M ALCOTT

found in my little book is owing to your interest in and encouragement of all my efforts from the first to the last, and if ever I can do anything to be proud of, my greatest happiness will be that I can thank you for that, as I may do for all the good there is in me.

In her journal, Louisa wrote of *Flower Fables:* "It has sold very well, and people seem to like it. I feel quite proud that the little tales that I wrote . . . when I was sixteen should now bring money and fame." It thrilled Louisa to think that people all over the country were now reading and enjoying her stories. But more importantly to her, she had found something she did well that could ease her family's financial stress. Louisa put all the money she earned into what she called the "Alcott Sinking Fund." Her hard-earned dollars were used to pay for groceries, emergencies, and unexpected expenses to keep the family from sinking into debt. Whenever there was any extra, Louisa spent it on little gifts and treats for her sisters.

LOVE AND SACRIFICE

In addition to her writing, Louisa continued to teach, sew, and take in laundry. Over time, she had become the leader and main breadwinner of the family. Her mother worked too many hours, trying to help too many people. No matter what Abba did, she realized that she couldn't solve everyone's problems. A sense of hopelessness overwhelmed her. Abba resigned from the city mission and never worked outside the home again. Now that he had fully recovered from smallpox and a near nervous breakdown, Bronson decided to try another lecture tour. He traveled around the country, speaking on transcendentalist philosophy. At first things went wonderfully well. He earned $150, which he proudly sent home to the family. Audiences were appreciative. Encouraged by their response, Bronson extended his tour another four months.

Louisa described his return to Boston in her journal:

In February Father came home. Paid his way, but no more. A dramatic scene when he arrived in the night . . . Mother flew down, crying 'My husband!' We rushed after, and five white figures embraced the half-frozen wanderer who came in hungry, tired, cold, and disappointed, but smiling bravely and as serene as ever. We fed and warmed and brooded over him, longing to ask if he had made any money, but no one did till little May said, after he had told the pleasant things, 'Well, did people pay you?' Then, with a queer look, he opened his pocketbook and showed one dollar, saying with a smile that made our eyes fill, 'Only that! My overcoat was stolen, and I had to buy a shawl. Many promises were not kept, and traveling is costly; but I have opened the way, and another year shall do better.'

I shall never forget how beautifully Mother answered him, though the dear, hopeful soul had built much on his success; but with a beaming face, she kissed him, saying, 'I call that doing *very well*. Since you are safely home, dear, we don't ask anything more.'

Anna and I choked down our tears, and took a little lesson in real love which we never forgot . . .

HAPPY MOMENTS

Louisa carried a lot of responsibility on her young shoulders, but her life was not all hard work. In Boston, the Alcotts were surrounded by Abba's extended family. They had more aunts, uncles, and cousins than they could count. Most of these relatives were very wealthy. The Mays couldn't really understand Bronson, but they loved Abba and the girls. They felt sorry for the family and their financial struggles. Often when Anna and Louisa went to work as governesses, they were caring for their relatives' children. The May women sent most of their sewing and mending to Louisa. They knew she needed the money. Whenever there were any extra concert tickets, they sent them to the Alcott house. Anna, Louisa, Lizzie, and May were often invited to stay with their relatives for weeks or even months at a time. In the spacious and comfortable May mansions, the Alcott girls experienced the pleasures of a life far different from their own. The four sisters were always included in the young people's picnics, parties, and plays. When the occasion called for it, their cousins gladly loaned them fancy dresses to wear. Louisa disliked being pitied. Sometimes she grew tired of being the "poor relation," of feeling shabby compared to the other girls. But they were all so kind, and they meant well. Louisa enjoyed being a part of their lively circle of friends. She loved going to the theater, the library, and museums. She thrived in sophisticated society.

When the Alcotts first moved to Boston, Louisa longed to return to her country life. She thought she couldn't live apart from the beauty of nature. But it turned out that she was a city girl after all.

The Lecture Circuit

In the days before radio, television, or the Internet, the lecture circuit was a popular source of entertainment and education. People attended lectures or speeches given by the most famous authors, politicians, scientists, and philosophers of the time. It was often their only opportunity to see these newsmakers in person. Sometimes organizers sold tickets to events and used the proceeds to pay the lecturer. Other events were free. The audience was asked to contribute to a collection for the guest speaker. Some of the most successful speakers during Bronson Alcott's day included Ralph Waldo Emerson, Mark Twain, and Susan B. Anthony.

Orchard House

In April of 1855, Louisa May Alcott was twenty-two years old. She wrote in her diary:

> I am in the garret with my papers round me, and a pile of apples to eat while I write my journal, plan stories, and enjoy the patter of the rain on the roof, in peace and quiet. Being behindhand, as usual, I'll make note of the main events up to date, for I don't waste ink in poetry and pages of rubbish now. I've begun to *live*, and have no time for sentimental musing . . .
>
> My book came out; and people began to think that topsey-turvey Louisa would amount to something after all, since she could do so well as housemaid, teacher, seamstress, and story-teller. Perhaps she may . . .

Summer plans are yet unsettled. Father wants to go to England: not a wise idea, I think. We shall probably stay here, and Anna and I go into the country as governesses. It's a queer way to live, but dramatic, and I rather like it; for we never know what is to come next . . .

Life was always hectic for the industrious Alcotts. Even though Abba had given up her official position at the mission, she remained active in community charity work. She took in boarders, or guests who rented rooms from the family. Often Abba's boarders were people with disabilities. She assisted them with their health care. Lizzie managed the housework. Bronson continued his lecture tours, to varying degrees of success. A gifted artist, May attended the prestigious School of Design. Anna and Louisa took jobs here, there, and everywhere. Anna worked for some time as the director of an asylum, or mental facility, in New York. Louisa preferred to stay in or around Boston. She loved the theater. She thought seriously about becoming a dramatic actress, performing on the professional stage. But in the end, Louisa decided to continue working as a teacher or nurse and companion. The Lovering family offered to pay Louisa $250 per year to be a governess to their daughter Alice. Louisa knew she would have her hands full with the spoiled and mischievous little girl, but compared to some other jobs, it was not so difficult. In addition, Louisa always had sewing to do. Her cousins had discovered that she was a talented dressmaker, and they were glad to give her the work. They also gave her their hand-me-downs: dresses that no longer suited them or were considered out of style. Louisa pulled the gowns apart and remade them into new dresses that her sisters were proud to wear. As she stitched away, she planned more stories she could sell to magazines.

A FAMILY TRAGEDY

The Alcotts were hardly ever together in one place anymore, but they remained very close at heart. Louisa's entire life revolved around her precious family. She revered her mother, whom she considered to be a saint. Her frustrations with her father were balanced with compassion and concern for his well-being. It was true that Bronson's high-minded principles and lofty ideals did not put food on the table. But Louisa knew her father was sincere in his convictions and in his steady belief that their situation would soon improve.

Louisa's sisters were her best friends. In her journals, she wrote with great affection of Anna or Nan, Elizabeth whom she called Lizzie, Betty, or Beth, and of course May. She was so proud of them.

In 1856, Lizzie and May came down with scarlet fever. Abba may have carried the infection home, after nursing the sick children of a poor immigrant family. For sixteen-year-old May, the symptoms were fairly mild. She recovered quickly. But Lizzie was twenty-one, and the fever had a much worse affect on her. All summer she battled a rash and raging fever. Her mother and sisters sat by her bedside, keeping a constant watch over her. There really wasn't anything else they could do. By the fall, the fever had subsided, yet Lizzie remained pale and sickly. She had lost her appetite and had grown very thin. As the family went back to work, Lizzie was always uppermost in their thoughts and prayers.

When Anna, Louisa, and May came home for the holidays, they were shocked by the changes they saw in their younger sister. A year later, Lizzie still had not regained her strength. She seemed even weaker than before. The doctors were at a loss to explain why she did not recover. Nothing that they had suggested made any improvement in her condition. They had no more treatments to offer. By the winter of 1857, to everyone's distress, it became clear that Lizzie was dying.

Louisa rushed home to be by her sister's side. Lizzie preferred Louisa's company to anyone else's. It comforted her to know that Louisa was nearby. Louisa described their time together in her journal: "Sad quiet days in her room, and strange nights keeping up the fire and watching the dear little shadow try to wile (sic) away the long sleepless hours without troubling me. She sews, reads, sings softly, and lies looking at the fire,—so sweet and patient and so worn. My heart is broken."

Not Much Help

In the 1800s, there were no hospitals, only "sanitariums." They were places more like the health spas or recovery centers of today. Doctors knew very little about the causes of common illnesses and infections. They didn't understand the importance of sterilizing equipment to prevent the spread of disease. There were no blood tests, x-rays, or scanning devices. Doctors could not see what was happening inside a patient's body. Even if they found the problem, there were very few effective medications or treatments to cure it.

Most of the popular "cures" of the time did more harm than good. Patients who were given opium and strychnine often lost their hair and teeth. Some suffered nerve damage from these drugs. Certain pain medications, such as morphine, proved to be terribly addictive. The application of bloodsucking leeches did not rid the body of infection. Instead, it left patients weak and vulnerable to disease.

Early in the morning of March 14, 1858, Lizzie lost her two-year battle with the mysterious illness. Abba and Louisa were with her when she died. The funeral service was very simple—just the Alcotts and a few of their closest friends. Ralph Waldo Emerson and Henry David Thoreau helped carry the casket to the cemetery.

Lizzie had always been quiet and shy. She stayed in the background, watching everyone else. She was content to share in their joys and sorrows without desiring any adventures of her own. Somehow her sweet presence brought peace to the home. Now the Alcotts' lives seemed empty without her.

THE FIRST WEDDING

A few months after Lizzie's death, Bronson and Abba moved back to Concord for good. They needed the comfort of being near their dearest friends, the Emersons, the Hawthornes, and Thoreau. With money from the sale of their previous home, and the help of a small inheritance from one of Abba's relatives, the Alcotts purchased a property they called Orchard House. Abba went to work decorating and furnishing the new home. Bronson busied himself with the renovations and landscaping. When they were finished, it was a charming place.

Louisa was relieved to see her parents comfortably settled at last. Over time, the community had forgotten its concerns about Bronson's educational philosophies, and he had adopted some more moderate views. Now he had been asked to serve as the superintendent of Concord's public schools, though Louisa would continue to be the main breadwinner of the family, a responsibility she treasured. It gave her great joy to provide for her loved ones.

Although Louisa had a bedroom at Orchard House, she rarely stayed at the home she affectionately called "Apple Slump." Louisa had decided that her place was in the city. She was a self-supporting young woman, with a successful career, something almost unheard of in her day. When she didn't live with the family of a pupil or a patient, she rented a room at a boardinghouse. Louisa preferred it that way. As a writer, she needed peace and quiet. She liked having her privacy. From autumn to spring, Louisa lived in Boston. She visited her parents often throughout the year, and she stayed with them during the summer.

By this time, a young man named John Pratt was well on his way to becoming a part of the Alcott family. The girls had seen him often at social events, including their cousins' picnics and parties. The young people frequently put on productions of Louisa's plays for fun. John eagerly joined the cast. He and Anna often played the romantic parts together. Somewhere along the way, they fell in love for real. Louisa liked John and approved of the match. Still, her heart ached when their engagement was announced. She wrote in her journal that John was "a true man—full of fine possibilities, but so modest one does not see it at

The Alcotts bought Orchard House and returned to Concord after Lizzie's death.

once . . . He is handsome, healthy, and happy . . . so full of love he is pleasant to look at. I moaned in private over my great loss, and said I'd never forgive John for taking Anna from me; but I shall if he makes her happy, and turn to my little May for my comfort." It seemed appropriate that as the oldest, Anna would be the first of the Alcott girls to marry. But Louisa hated the thought of "losing" another sister. Marriage would inevitably change their relationship.

Louisa herself was bright, attractive, intelligent, and quick-witted. She had quite a few admirers of her own, but none that was capable of winning her affection. Louisa relished her freedom and independence too much to give it up for just anyone. As she described Anna's wedding in her journal, she teased: "Mr. Emerson kissed her; and I thought that honor would make even matrimony endurable, for he is the god of my idolatry, and has been for years."

But the prospect of a congratulatory kiss from her hero was not truly enough to persuade Louisa to abandon her ambitions. As she grew older, she grew more determined than ever to make her mark on the world.

John Pratt fell in love with Louisa's sister Anna. Louisa was happy for the couple, but a bit sad over the change in her relationship with her sister.

A COUNTRY AT WAR

For the past several years, the Alcotts had devoted much of their time and energy to overcoming the challenges their own family faced. However, they were not oblivious to what was going on in the world around them. On the contrary, they were very concerned about the crisis their country faced.

Sharp disagreements had arisen between the Northern and Southern states. One cause of disagreement was slavery. For hundreds of years, African people had been kidnapped from their homes, brought to the United States, and sold as slaves. In the South, farmers grew large quantities of cotton and other crops. They depended on slave labor to help them run their vast plantations. In the Northern states, more people worked in factories or on small family farms. They did not have the same need for slave labor. Many people in the North believed that slavery was wrong. They decided to make slavery illegal in their states, and they tried to force the South to do the same. As more of the western territories became states, there was tension over whether they would become "free" or "slave" states. There was also disagreement about slaves who escaped to the North or to the West. Should people living in free states be compelled to return these slaves to their "owners" in the South?

Not everyone in the South supported slavery. But many believed in "state's rights," the idea that each state had the right to make its own laws. They believed that the national government should not make decisions for them and should not make laws without each state's approval. People living in the Southern states grew angry at the federal government. They felt that the government made laws that treated them unfairly. In 1860,

South Carolina announced that it would secede from the union. It would no longer be a part of the United States of America. The Northern states insisted that South Carolina did not have the right to secede. They wanted the president to send armies to South Carolina to take control of the state. South Carolina wanted the rest of the Southern states to join it in forming a new country, the Confederate States of America.

Bronson and Abba Alcott had always taught their daughters that slavery was wrong. They signed petitions and participated in demonstrations against slavery. They boycotted products made with slave labor. With great sadness, the family listened to speakers who had witnessed the horrors of slavery. They read newspaper reports detailing the atrocities committed against slaves in the South. The Alcotts did what they could to make a difference in their own community. Although most of their Northern neighbors opposed slavery, it did not necessarily mean that they believed blacks and whites should have equal rights. People tended to view cultural differences as evidence that the African American race was seen as inferior. The Alcotts' belief in racial equality seemed radical at the time.

Years earlier, Bronson had accepted a black student at the Temple School, a controversial decision that cost him his job. Yet he refused to compromise his principles. Historians credit Bronson with preventing a bloody riot in Boston when conflict broke out over the return of a runaway slave. He stepped forward into the fray and calmly and silently led the overzealous "citizen's army" to walk away from a battle with armed police officers. During her time at the mission, Abba taught reading and writing to African American adults three nights a week. Louisa served as her assistant.

In Concord, the Alcotts were friends with many of the leaders of the abolitionist movement. They knew the legendary Harriet Tubman, a former slave who had organized an escape route for other runaways known as the Underground Railroad. The Alcotts also attended a series of meetings featuring the fiery speeches of a man named John Brown. During his visit to the New England states, Brown proposed a violent protest, a slave rebellion, leading to the formation of a new United States. Not long afterward, he was hanged for launching an assault on a federal armory at Harpers Ferry, Virginia. Brown's widow and widowed daughter-in-law came to stay with the Alcotts at Orchard House.

Just like her parents, Louisa May Alcott became an ardent abolitionist. Nothing stirred up Louisa's fighting spirit more than the thought of injustice. She had always been the one to rescue her friends and family from any kind of suffering, whether emotional, physical, or financial. Whenever she saw someone being misjudged or mistreated, her first impulse was to rush to their defense. When the Civil War broke out, Alcott was eager to do her part in the fight for freedom.

John Brown led a raid on Harpers Ferry, Virginia, in 1859. He and his supporters captured the federal armory and took over the town for a short while until federal troops and local militia defeated them.

The Underground Railroad

African American slaves longed to be free. But no matter how badly they were treated, it was against the law for them to leave their owners. Still, many dared to run away. If only they could make it to one of the Northern states, where slavery was illegal, they would be free. But slave owners were reluctant to lose their valuable "property." They went looking for those who escaped. Runaways who got caught faced unspeakably cruel punishment or even death.

The Underground Railroad was a loosely organized system made up of volunteers, both whites and free blacks, who wanted to help fugitive slaves on their journey. They used code words for their secret operations. Runaways were called "passengers" and their guides were called "conductors." Homes that sheltered escaped slaves were known as "stations." Between 1840 and 1860, thousands of courageous men and women followed the Underground Railroad to freedom.

Harriet Tubman (far left) was an important leader of the Underground Railroad.

135,000 SETS, 270,000 VOLUMES SOLD.

UNCLE TOM'S CABIN

FOR SALE HERE.

AN EDITION FOR THE MILLION, COMPLETE IN 1 Vol., PRICE 37 1-2 CENTS.
" " IN GERMAN, IN 1 Vol., PRICE 50 CENTS.
" " IN 2 Vols,. CLOTH, 6 PLATES, PRICE $1.50.
SUPERB ILLUSTRATED EDITION, IN 1 Vol., WITH 153 ENGRAVINGS,
PRICES FROM $2.50 TO $5.00.

The Greatest Book of the Age.

Uncle Tom's Cabin was a wildly successful book, which helped advance

"I Can't Fight, But I Can Nurse!"

One of Alcott's favorite books was *Uncle Tom's Cabin* by Harriet Beecher Stowe. This popular novel exposed the evils of slavery through powerful storytelling. It inspired Alcott to use the same technique to communicate her own convictions. She had been making quite a bit of money writing murder mysteries and gothic thrillers, as well as fairy tales and love stories. Now she would try writing stories that were more than entertainment. She wanted to write stories that would make people think. For the first time, Alcott wrote stories that explored subjects such as slavery, equality, and interracial relationships. Some magazines felt these new stories were too controversial to publish, but others were willing to print them. Alcott wrote a poem mourning the death of John Brown. It appeared in the abolitionist journal, *The Liberator*.

Alcott's participation in the war effort was not limited to writing. In her free time, she sewed uniforms for the new Union army. She stitched blankets and cut strips of cloth to roll into bandages. Still, Alcott wanted to do more. She wished she could join the brave young soldiers marching into battle, but women were not allowed near the front. As the fighting raged on, the government called for volunteers to nurse the thousands of

Harriet Beecher Stowe

She described herself as simply "a wife and mother." However, Harriet Beecher Stowe was also one of the most prominent and successful authors of the nineteenth century. In 1851, Stowe wrote *Uncle Tom's Cabin*, a novel about the brutality of slavery. The book quickly sold more than a million copies and was translated into twenty languages. For the first time, many people began to think about the injustice of slavery. They demanded an end to the evil practice. In 1862, Stowe was introduced to President Abraham Lincoln. He greeted her by saying, "So you are the little woman who wrote the book that started this great war!"

wounded men who were quickly filling up the makeshift "hospitals." To Alcott, it was a welcome invitation. "I can't fight," she said, "but I can nurse!"

LOUISA GOES TO WASHINGTON

In those days, the word "nurse" could describe anyone who took care of a sick person. So at thirty years old, Alcott had some experience in nursing. She had been Lizzie's constant companion during the last few months of her life. She had helped other members of her family whenever they suffered an illness of some kind. She had also worked as a nurse or companion to several invalids, people whose illness confined them to bed.

In England, a woman named Florence Nightingale was just beginning to create a standard of care and a system for training professional nurses. To prepare for her wartime assignment, Alcott carefully studied Nightingale's groundbreaking book, *Notes on Nursing.* On December 11,

Florence Nightingale was a pioneer in the field of nursing.

1862, Alcott was told to report to the Union Hotel Hospital at George-town in Washington, D.C. She packed her trunk with the dark-colored dresses all nurses were required to wear. Alcott also took a copper teakettle and her pen and paper. As she wrapped her belongings, Alcott thought about how bored and lonely the recovering soldiers would be. She filled the remaining space in her trunk with items she could use to amuse her patients: games they could play and books she could read to them.

When Alcott reported for duty, she was horrified by the condition of the "hospital." The building had been a luxury hotel, hastily converted to a ward for wounded soldiers. By the time Alcott arrived, the place was absolutely filthy. The air reeked with the stench of sickness and death, in part because all the windows had been boarded up to prevent theft. When food, medicine, or blood spilled on the floor, it was immediately absorbed into the thick carpeting. Little could be done to clean it.

The head nurse showed Alcott to a tiny bedroom she would share with another volunteer. The training consisted of a few brief instructions. Alcott was taught how to make up the patients' beds and how to wash their hands and faces regularly with strong soap. She learned that she would be responsible for changing her patients' clothing once a week, emptying their bedpans, and dispensing whatever medication the doctor prescribed. Occasionally she might be asked to assist a doctor in surgery, handing him his instruments or holding the patient still. (When supplies ran out, the doctors had to operate without anesthetic.) Whenever she could, Alcott applied what she had learned from Nightingale's book. Her patients grew very fond of her. Alcott was so warm, friendly, and cheerful.

A DAY AT THE HOSPITAL

In January of 1863, Alcott wrote in her journal:

> I never began the year in a stranger place than this; five hundred miles from home, alone among strangers, doing painful duties all day long, and leading a life of constant excitement in this greathouse surrounded by three or four hundred men in all stages of suffering, disease and death. Though often home sick, heart sick, and worn out, I like it—find real pleasure in comforting, tending and cheering these poor souls who seem to love me, to feel my sympathy though unspoken, and acknowledge my hearty good will in spite of the ignorance, awkwardness, and bashfulness which I cannot help showing in so new and trying a situation . . .
>
> I shall record the events of a day as a sample of the days I spend—
>
> Up at six, dress by gas light, run through my ward and fling up the windows though the men grumble and shiver; but the air is bad enough to breed a pestilence and as no notice is taken of our frequent appeals for ventilation I must do what I can. Poke up the fire, add blankets, joke, coax, and command . . . I trot, trot, giving out rations, cutting up food for helpless "boys," washing faces, teaching my attendants how beds are made or floors swept, dressing wounds, taking Dr. Fitzpatrick's orders, (privately wishing all the time that he would be more gentle with my big babies,) dusting tables, sewing bandages, keeping my tray tidy, rushing up and down after pillows, bed linen, sponges, books and directions, till it seems as if I would joyfully pay down all I possess for fifteen minutes rest . . .

The answering of letters from friends after someone has died is the saddest and hardest duty a nurse has to do . . . At nine the bell rings, gas is turned down and day nurses go to bed. Night nurses go on duty, and sleep and death have the house to themselves.

Shortly after her arrival, Alcott was assigned to the night shift herself. This change of schedule suited her perfectly. Things were much quieter at night. She had time to reflect on her experiences and the people whose lives she touched. New story ideas were brewing in her head. Among so many dying men, she could not help but think of her beloved teacher, Henry David Thoreau. After a long battle with illness, Thoreau had died that summer. He had only been forty-five years old. One night, while on duty, Alcott composed a beautiful, heartfelt poem in memory of her dear friend. She called it "Thoreau's Flute."

When Alcott came off-duty, it was daylight. She could take a few hours to explore the nation's capital city. She visited the monuments, museums, and libraries. Then it was back to the hospital to sleep before her next shift.

HOME AGAIN

In spite of Alcott's efforts to protect herself and her patients from infection, she soon came down with a terrible cough. At first she ignored her symptoms and went about her work. She thought she had a common cold. In reality, Alcott had contracted typhoid, a disease that could prove fatal. When she showed signs of a fever, the hospital doctors sent her to bed immediately.

Every part of Alcott's body ached. No matter how many clothes or blankets they piled on her, she was always shivering. Her mouth broke out in painful sores. She slipped in and out of consciousness. Day after day, her condition grew worse. She was on the verge of dying. In a desperate attempt to save her life, doctors prescribed huge doses of calomel, a mercury chloride medication they hoped would purge her system of the infection. Alcott experienced terrible hallucinations. She dreamed she was being chased by giant surgical instruments or that she had millions of patients to care for and could never get to them all. One day,

Dorothea Dix

Dorothea Dix had great compassion for those forgotten or neglected by society. She worked for more than forty years to provide better treatment for people with mental illnesses and to improve the conditions of the nation's prisons. When the Civil War began, Dix volunteered her services to the Union army. She was appointed Superintendent of Female Nurses and was put in charge of all women nurses in Union hospitals.

Extremely organized and efficient, Dix instituted strict requirements for all prospective nurses. She would tolerate no giddy girls in search of adventure or romance. To be accepted into service, volunteers had to be plain, hardworking women over the age of thirty. The superintendent had a stern demeanor that did not make her very popular. (The nurses called her "Dragon Dix.") But under her leadership, the quality of nursing care was greatly improved.

Alcott awoke briefly to see her grief-stricken father standing by her bed. Not knowing if she would survive the illness, the hospital staff had called her family to come for her.

With all the other patients to attend to, the doctors and nurses could not properly care for Alcott. Bronson gently nursed his ailing daughter in the hospital dormitory until she could be safely moved. On January 21, 1863, only forty days after she arrived at the hospital, Alcott had to be sent home. She was still barely conscious. Nursing Superintendent Dorothea Dix packed up Alcott's belongings for her. Dix also put together a gift basket with tea and medicine, a blanket and pillow, some perfume, and a small Bible.

Later on, Alcott remembered very little of the train ride to Concord or the weeks that followed. At Orchard House, Bronson and Abba kept a desperate watch. They feared they were about to lose another daughter. It took Alcott a long time to fight off the fever and regain her strength, but at last she did. She would always have some lingering effects. For years to come she experienced pains and illnesses that were related to her bout with typhoid—side effects of the medication she had been given. She had pain in her joints and numbness in her arms and legs. Her cough never completely went away. She was often hoarse and lost her voice. She suffered vertigo, or dizzy spells, that sent her to bed for weeks at a time.

PICKING UP HER PEN

During her illness, Alcott received countless letters, cards, and gifts from her friends and relatives. She was encouraged by their love and prayers. On March 22, Alcott felt well enough to leave her room for the first time. She started taking short walks and carriage rides, which refreshed her. She now found joy in the simplest everyday activities. "To go very near death teaches one to value life," she observed.

Within a week, Alcott had even more reason to rejoice. Bronson came home from a trip to Boston to report that Anna had given birth to her first child, a baby boy named Frederick Alcott Pratt. Louisa wrote a teasing letter to her older sister, demanding to know "Where is my *niece*?" Anna had promised her a little girl, who would be her namesake. Of course, all of the Alcotts were truly thrilled by the news. "We opened our mouths and screamed for about two minutes," Louisa told Anna. "Then mother began to cry, I to laugh, and May to pour out questions . . . Father had told everyone he met, from Emerson to the coach driver." Aunt Louisa went to work at once, sewing pretty baby clothes for her precious nephew.

As Alcott regained her strength, she began to think about returning to work. While at the hospital, she had received word that "Pauline's Passion and Punishment" had won a $100 prize in a short-story contest. The government then sent her $10 for the six weeks she served at the hospital. Due to her illness, Alcott had no other income. Predictably, the family's finances were now in grave condition. Debts had accumulated, Orchard House required repairs, and May needed a new wardrobe. So Alcott picked up her pen to write again.

With a full and sometimes heavy heart, she began writing a series of essays on her experience at the army hospital. She told moving stories about her brave patients and the suffering they endured. Alcott's *Hospital Sketches* were published one at a time in *The Boston Commonwealth*. They were an enormous success. Several publishers competed for the right to print the sketches in book form. To Alcott's immense satisfaction, the

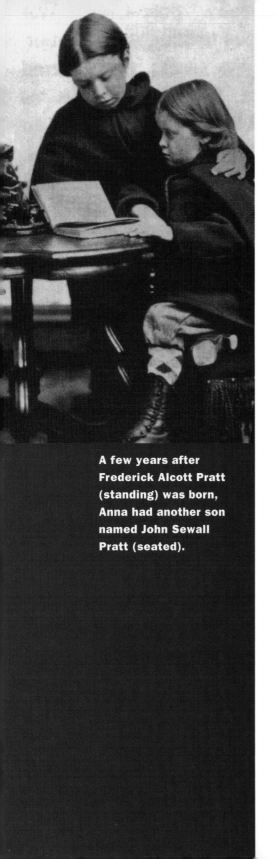

A few years after Frederick Alcott Pratt (standing) was born, Anna had another son named John Sewall Pratt (seated).

competitors included the company that employed James T. Fields, the man who told her she couldn't write. Alcott carefully considered the offers and chose the best one. She made arrangements for part of the proceeds to go to a fund for war orphans.

Although *Sketches* had been written under the pen name "Tribulation Periwinkle," everyone soon knew the real author was Louisa May Alcott. Alcott became a celebrity of sorts, especially among the people of Boston and Concord, her two hometowns. In addition to the accolades and attention, Alcott discovered another benefit that came from success. In the past she had written stories and submitted them to magazines in the hopes that they would be published, as they often were. Now magazine editors were coming to *her*, begging her to write for them.

SEVEN

The Miss Alcott

In 1863, Alcott cheerfully recorded in her journal that she had earned more than $600 ($15,000 in today's economy) for her stories. It was a significant amount, as much as a secretary or seamstress might make, and almost three times as much as any teacher. She had become a regular contributor to several magazines. Her editors routinely gave her assignments and payment in advance. Under a variety of pen names, Alcott wrote comedy, drama, romance, fantasy, and adventure. She also wrote more dark thrillers for the magazines that preferred them. To these sensational stories, she signed her name "A. M. Barnard."

For several years, Alcott had been working on a novel inspired by a favorite quote from Emerson: "Life is a train of moods like a string of beads; and as we pass through them they prove to be many colored lenses, which paint the world their own hue, and each shows us only what lies in its own focus." Alcott's book, *Moods*, explored the many moods of her heroine, Sylvia.

Alcott knew that the frivolous stories she wrote for magazines could hardly be considered classical literature. She herself teasingly referred to them as "rubbish." However, this new book was her "real" work of fiction, her first serious contribution to the literary world. Alcott spent months at a time developing its themes. When she finally showed the book to her publishers, they told her it was too long. They pointed out that parts of the plot were confusing. They told her they might be interested in publishing the book if she would cut the length substantially. At first, Alcott refused to make any drastic changes. She had already done quite a bit of editing. This was one story she had written to please herself. Alcott put the manuscript away for a while and concentrated on other projects. Then one day, she suddenly thought of a way to completely reorganize the novel. The new structure would eliminate ten chapters. By the time she finished the revision, it was not quite the book she had hoped it would be. Yet her publishers seemed very pleased.

Moods was released on Christmas Day, 1864. Alcott held her breath and waited to see how it would be received. This was the first book she had published since people recognized her as "Tribulation Periwinkle." It was her first full-length novel. To her great relief, Alcott saw that literary critics gave *Moods* good reviews. All over town Alcott found friends and neighbors reading the book. They were raving about it. By New Year's Day, the first printing had completely sold out. Her book was officially a success, and Alcott had established herself as a legitimate author.

MOVING ON

In between other writing projects, Alcott still found time to write short stories that advocated the abolition of slavery. Not every magazine would publish these political works, but some did. Due to her ongoing health problems, Alcott could not return to nursing wounded soldiers in the army hospitals. However, she *could* sew more blankets, bandages, and uniforms. To raise money for the hospitals and other types of relief work, Alcott dramatized a series of scenes from Dickens's work for the stage. The performances were put on by the Tremont Theatre Company in Boston. They brought in more than $2,500, which Alcott donated to the war effort.

On April 9, 1865, the Confederate general Robert E. Lee surrendered his troops to the Union general Ulysses S. Grant at Appomattox Court House, Virginia. The Civil War was over at last. The city of Boston erupted into cheers at the news. The Alcotts gladly joined their friends and neighbors in celebration. Five days later, they were stunned to learn of President Lincoln's assassination.

The war officially ended when General Robert E. Lee surrendered to General Ulysses S. Grant.

It seemed as though all of the Alcotts (and the Pratts) were seriously ill over the course of the next year. Members of the family traveled back and forth between Boston and Concord to take turns nursing each other. The month of June brought them some joy, as Anna gave birth to a second boy, John Sewall Pratt. Then in July, Louisa was invited to tour Europe with the invalid daughter of a wealthy Boston merchant. Ever since she was a little girl, Alcott had dreamed of traveling abroad. All the truly great authors had done so. Alcott wanted to see the cities and castles and cathedrals that had inspired her favorite writers. Perhaps they would inspire her, too. Mr. Weld offered to pay all of her travel expenses if she would assist young Anna. Alcott could barely contain her excitement.

Unfortunately, the trip turned out to be somewhat of a disappointment. Alcott got miserably seasick on the long ocean voyage. Her patient

An End to Slavery

On September 22, 1862, President Abraham Lincoln issued the Emancipation Proclamation. He declared that as of January 1, 1863, "all persons held as slaves . . . shall be then, thenceforward and forever free." The proclamation did not immediately put an end to slavery. The practice was already illegal in the North. Of course the Southern states had seceded from the Union. They no longer acknowledged or accepted President Lincoln's authority over them. But when the war ended, the Southern states were readmitted into the Union. They became subject to federal law. Slavery was then completely abolished.

complained a good deal about her aches and pains. Anna Weld rarely felt well. The young woman had no interest in sightseeing; she wanted nothing more than to rest at a series of European spas. After supporting herself for the past few years, Alcott found it frustrating to be an employee again. She had no say in where they went or what they did. The trip was

Depart/Arrive Boston
1/24 - Liverpool
2/23 - London
3 - Dover
4 - Ostende
5 - Brussels
6 - Cologne
7 - Koblenz
8 - Biebrich
9 - Schwalbach
10 - Wiesbaden
11 - Frankfurt
12 - Heidelberg
13 - Baden-Baden
14 - Freiburg
15 - Basel
16 - Berne
17 - Fribourg
18 - Lausanne
19 - Vevey
20 - Geneva
21 - Nice
22 - Paris

Alcott did not enjoy her trip to Europe as much as she hoped, but she did get to visit a number of interesting places and met unusual people during her travels. This map shows where Alcott went on her trip.

not a total disaster. Louisa and Anna got along well enough. When Anna *was* feeling better, they attended plays and parties. There were moments when Alcott could slip away and explore on her own. She got a taste of art, history, and culture that inspired her. At the luxurious health resorts that Miss Weld preferred, Alcott met some fascinating people, such as aristocrats, diplomats, and wealthy tourists from all over the world. Many of these quirky characters would appear in Alcott's stories later on. But after a full year of traveling, she had had enough. Alcott missed her family and her life in Boston. She couldn't wait to get home.

IN SEARCH OF SECURITY

Returning from Europe after a year's absence, Louisa looked at her parents with a fresh perspective. Bronson seemed his usual serene self, but Abba looked weak and sickly. They were getting older. Louisa could see her parents had less energy, and less interest in and ability to manage their own affairs. As usual, money was tight. Louisa needed to get back to work. "I dread debt more than the devil!" she exclaimed. Alcott found her publishers eager for more of her stories. Working day and night, she completed twelve new tales in three months. That year she earned $1,200 in royalties and other payments. It was hard work, but she quickly replenished the "Alcott Sinking Fund." Later, she asked a cousin to help her invest some of her savings. The family was comfortable enough, but Alcott worried about the future. Alcott wanted her family to be financially secure, even if she wasn't able to keep writing at such a frantic pace. Writing at all hours had begun to take a toll on her health. Ever since her bout with typhoid, she had been susceptible to illness and infection.

About this time, a publisher called H. B. Fuller asked Alcott to become the new editor of his children's magazine, *Merry's Museum*. She would be responsible for writing one story and one editorial a month, as well as reading other authors' manuscripts and choosing which ones to print. Other than *Flower Fables*, most of Alcott's previous stories had been written for adults. She didn't know if she really had the aptitude to write for children or edit a national magazine. The publisher was offering her a generous salary of $500 per year. Alcott decided she was willing to give it a try.

Alcott's financial stress evaporated immediately. Her salary was more than enough for her to live on, and it would help her take care of all of her parents' pressing needs. Alcott moved into her own apartment in Boston, so that she would have peace and quiet in which to write. She even took a little of her money and spent it on herself, decorating her rooms with the first furniture she had ever owned. In addition to her work on *Merry's Museum*, Alcott sold more than twenty-five stories and another book of fairy tales. After a while, May came to live with her.

With Lizzie gone and Anna busy with John and the children, Louisa and May had grown very close. For years, May had flitted from place to place, a perpetual student of the arts.

After years of wandering, May Alcott settled in Boston and taught art classes.

Louisa lovingly called her "our Raphael." Now May was ready to settle down and take on some responsibility. She began teaching art classes in Boston and Concord.

LITTLE WOMEN

Thomas Niles worked for Roberts Brothers publishers. The company had produced a very successful series of novels for boys. Now Niles was looking for a similar type series for girls. He had trouble finding the right kind of story. Most books written for girls were either fairy tales or preachy moral fables. The heroines were always sickeningly sweet and impossibly perfect. Niles wanted a book with an engaging story for and about "typical American girls."

Niles asked Louisa May Alcott to consider writing such a novel. She politely declined. While working on *Merry's Museum*, she realized she did have a gift for writing children's stories. However, she knew she had not been a "typical American girl" herself. She was not sure what "typical" girls would like. She would much rather write for boys. Niles pressed her to think about his request and he repeated it so often that Alcott eventually gave in. She had no idea that the novel she was so reluctant to write would become an American classic and make her a world-famous author.

Alcott decided to use a *Pilgrim's Progress* theme. She would tell the stories of four sisters and the life lessons they learned on their journey to adulthood. The only girls Alcott had ever been close to were her sisters. Naturally, they became the models for the book's characters. With her family's blessing, Alcott turned Anna into "Meg," the prim and proper older sister who often mothered her siblings. Lizzie became "Beth," sweet and shy. Switching around the letters of May's name, Alcott created "Amy," an aspiring artist and the undisputed beauty of the family. Alcott wrote herself in as "Jo," a lovable tomboy, with a knack for getting into scrapes. The girls' neighbor "Laurie" was actually a combination of two of Alcott's friends, Ladislas Wisniewski and Alf Whitman. The girls' father was off fighting in the war and absent from the family, as Bronson had often been. So the "March" family was headed up by "Marmee," who bore a striking resemblance to Abba.

Alcott poured all of her best memories of her childhood into this story. She also shared some of the hardships and difficulties, though she softened them a good deal. The plays she and her sisters performed, their little post office, the Pickwick Society, the rich relatives who could be kind or condescending, John and Anna's romance, Lizzie's death—Alcott relived all these experiences and hundreds more. She tenderly wove these real-life people, places, and events into her story, adding touches of truth to every page.

When she completed the 405-page manuscript, Alcott wasn't sure how well she had done. After writing countless murder mysteries, gothic fairy tales, and melodramatic romances, Alcott felt that her new book seemed a little dull. Thomas Niles agreed. However, he had the good

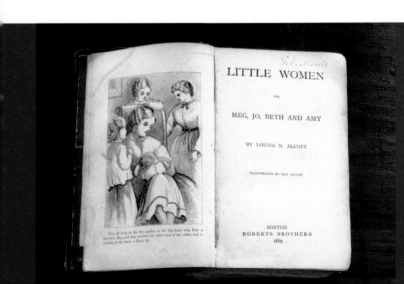

Little Women was a huge success. Louisa's sister May created the illustration on the left shown here in the first edition of the book.

sense to realize that as an elderly bachelor, he was not the best judge of these things. He gave a few chapters to his niece and her friends. The girls absolutely loved it and demanded to see the rest of the story at once. There was something very appealing about the simple story. The girls could relate to the characters, who were in many ways just like them. They couldn't wait to find out what happened to Meg, Jo, Beth, and Amy. It was a sign of things to come.

Little Women was published in September of 1868. It became an instant best seller. Little girls all over the world raved about their new favorite book and its wonderful author. In New England, Louisa was now known as "*The* Miss Alcott." She would never have to worry about providing for her family again.

Louisa's Boys

Louisa May Alcott never married, though as a young girl she dreamed of finding true love. Alcott grew up to be bright, spirited, and passionate about her convictions. Few men could measure up to her high ideals. Over the years, there were a number of boys whose wit and charm engaged her—schoolmates, neighbors, friends. Alcott adored these young men. But the affection she felt for her "dear boys" more closely resembled that of a mother or older sister. Their relationships never led to romance. Instead, they remained lifelong friends.

By the time she reached her late thirties, Alcott realized that she led a rich and full life as it was. She had a successful and rewarding career, a close and loving family, and all the freedom and independence she had longed for as a little girl. She wouldn't trade it for anything.

EIGHT

"The Children's Friend"

As a teenager, Louisa May Alcott had vowed to be "rich and famous and happy" before she died. At the age of thirty-six, Alcott realized that her dreams had come true. With the phenomenal success of *Little Women*, Alcott became a household name. She received hundreds of fan letters from her young readers. They flocked to Concord to see Orchard House, the real setting of the March family home. Newspaper reporters followed Alcott all over the city, begging for interviews. Anytime she appeared in public, she was asked for her autograph. Photographers snapped pictures while artists quickly sketched her likeness.

Like Louisa May Alcott, Frances Hodgson Burnett was another successful children's book author.

Everywhere she went, Alcott was the toast of the town. Like her parents before her, she could count some of the most famous and influential people of her day among her circle of friends. At banquets and receptions, she found herself in the company of other renowned children's book authors such as Mary Mapes Dodge (*Hans Brinker, or The Silver Skates*) and Frances Hodgson Burnett (*The Secret Garden, The Little Princess*). Alcott had a busy social life. She could go to lectures, concerts, theaters, and museums as often as she liked without having to wait for a relative to donate an extra ticket.

Perhaps the most gratifying thing for Alcott about being a famous writer was that publishers could not get enough of her work. There were no more rejections. Everything Alcott wrote made it into print, including articles, essays, poems, plays, and short stories. She was even asked to contribute to an advice column for a newspaper. Occasionally, Alcott experimented with writing novels for adults on more dark and complex themes. They were critically acclaimed. But her children's novels were considered her masterpieces. Always prolific,

Alcott practically wrote one a year, every year, for the rest of her life. Several of these were sequels to *Little Women*, like *Little Men* and *Jo's Boys*. Other popular titles included *An Old Fashioned Girl*, *Eight Cousins*, and *Rose in Bloom*. Each new book sold hundreds of thousands of copies.

With her royalty checks, Alcott paid off all of her family's debts, and then some. She took great delight in being able to shower them with gifts, especially the luxuries they had gone without over the years. Alcott hired servants to take over the cooking and cleaning at Orchard House so that Abba wouldn't be troubled with it. When her parents were ill, in addition to waiting on them herself, Alcott hired nurses to supervise their care. Bronson benefited from his daughter's celebrity in some unexpected ways. Publishers agreed to print two of his philosophical books, out of respect for Louisa. When Bronson went out to lecture, he found audiences much more responsive to his talks. It helped to be introduced as "the Father of *Little Women*."

Louisa also kept May in fashionable clothes and provided financial support as she needed it. She made generous contributions to her nephews' college funds.

For herself, Alcott was glad no longer to be a "poor relation" dressed in someone else's hand-me-downs. With her trunks packed full of lovely silk dresses, she planned another trip to Europe. This time, May accompanied her. Alcott loved being able to go wherever she wanted to go and see whatever she wanted to see. She arrived as a famous American author, not as an invalid's nursemaid. In each country, she received a warm welcome from her fans. The two sisters visited cathedrals, castles, and monuments to their hearts' content. They took long walks through lovely parks and quaint little shopping districts. They went to the theater, to the opera, to elaborate balls and parties. May loved touring the museums, sketching and painting her own masterpieces. Louisa took notes for future poems, stories, and books.

YOURS FOR REFORM

Alcott discovered that her fame gave her a great platform from which to express her views. She could use her influence to effect change in her community, in her country, and maybe even the world. An ardent abolitionist before the Civil War, Alcott continued to crusade for racial equality

May drew this picture of the hotel room the two sisters shared in Paris.

afterward. Like her mother, she cared deeply for those less fortunate. She was also passionate about women's rights.

Alcott was the first woman in Concord to vote in a school board election. It would be another forty years before a constitutional amendment would grant women the right to vote in national elections, but that didn't keep Alcott and her peers from voicing their opinions about the political process. She signed her correspondences "Yours for Reform," and later "Yours for all kinds of reform."

Alcott began speaking at rallies and special events, but she said the most with her pen. The author used her stories to communicate with

An illustration shows women trying to vote. It would be years before the Nineteenth Amendment would give women the right to vote.

her audience on both an emotional and intellectual level. Alcott's heroines were women of courage, strength, and character. They refused to compromise their principles. These heroines did not succumb to pressure from society or let what was expected of them dictate their actions. They valued faith and family. They married for love, not money—if they married at all. They were committed to making a difference in their world. By today's standards, Alcott's values seem conservative, perhaps even "traditional." To her young readers, however, they were anything but!

SAYING GOOD-BYE

Charles Dickens, one of Alcott's favorite authors, once began a novel with the memorable line "It was the best of times, it was the worst of times." He could have been describing Alcott's later years. So many wonderful things had happened, and so many of her dreams had come true. And yet she also suffered painful losses and personal tragedies.

While in Europe, one morning Louisa and May picked up an English language newspaper and learned that their brother-in-law, John Pratt, had died after a brief illness. John and Anna had only been married for ten years. Their son Freddie was eight, and Johnny was six. John had been a marvelous husband and father. Louisa's heart ached for her sister and her precious nephews. She determined to devote all the royalties from *Little Men* to help support them. She promised to "be a father" to the boys, playing rowdy, rough-and-tumble games with them and teaching them to play ball.

The good-byes were just beginning. Years of long hours and hard work had taken their toll on Abba Alcott. Her health had gradually deteriorated. She had been an invalid for the better part of a decade. In 1877, she suffered through a long and painful illness before dying in Louisa's arms.

Soon after, while living on her own in London, May met a Swiss banker named Ernest Nieriker. Although May was thirty-eight and Ernest only twenty-two, the couple fell in love and were married in London in 1878. May could not contain her joy. She begged Louisa to

May's husband, Ernest, is featured in this painting of their Paris apartment by May.

come for a visit and celebrate with her. For one reason after another, Louisa had to postpone her trip. Soon the family received word that May was expecting a baby. Louisa May Nieriker was born in Paris on November 8, 1879. Baby "Lulu" was happy and healthy, but May struggled to regain her strength after childbirth. She came down with meningitis.

On December 29 in Concord, Louisa May Alcott returned home from running errands to find dear old Mr. Emerson waiting for her. Tears were streaming down his face. Emerson had received a telegram from Ernest Nieriker, asking him to tell the Alcotts that May had died. May had known her husband would have a hard time raising a tiny baby by himself. He couldn't work and care for the child at the same time. She needed a mother. May left little Lulu to her sister's care.

After her sister's death, Louisa adopted her niece, Lulu.

MISS ALCOTT'S BABY

Alcott was devastated by her sister's death, but she could only grieve for so long. Ernest Nieriker honored his wife's wishes and sent Lulu to the United States to be raised by her namesake, Aunt Louisa. At the age of forty-eight, Alcott found she had become a mother. The adorable little blonde haired, blue-eyed baby reminded Louisa so much of May. Yet Lulu proved to have Louisa's ("Aunt Wee's") independent spirit. Alcott fell in love with her at once and began the process of spoiling her. She wrote a letter to Bronson describing Lulu's first birthday party:

> The little queen in her high chair sat and looked with delight at the tiny cake with *one* candle burning in it, picture books, flowers, a doll, silver mug, rattle with bells, and some gay cards . . . . She seemed quite over powered by her feelings and sung, laughted, [sic] and called 'Up ! Bow wow, Mama Da,' and all her little words, in great glee. Then she chose the picture book and was absorbed by it like a true artist's baby.

Lulu filled Alcott's home with love and laughter. The whole family was comforted by her presence.

PAYING A PRICE

Years earlier, at the Union army hospital, Alcott had been given large doses of a medicine called calomel. Doctors didn't realize that it could cause mercury poisoning and other complications. Alcott's immune system never really recovered from her bout with typhoid. Long hours at her desk and the hectic pace of her daily life also took its toll on her health. Throughout her forties and into her fifties, Alcott routinely experienced physical setbacks. One day her rheumatism or arthritis would bother her. The following week she'd developed a terrible cough or cold or sore throat. Her legs throbbed so that she could hardly walk, or her shoulder ached so badly that she had to wear a sling. Doctors gave her painkillers to try: opium and morphine. They had no idea that these were both highly addictive drugs. For years Alcott tried every possible cure, from diet and exercise, to medication, to "mind cures" and electric shock therapy. Nothing helped. She only got worse.

When she wasn't able to care for her, Louisa sent Lulu to stay with her Aunt Anna and her cousins, Freddie and Johnnie Pratt. By the end of 1887, Alcott's health problems were constant. Her digestive system started to shut down, and she could no longer tolerate food. No one knew whether this was somehow a side effect of her medication or a symptom of disease. She may have had cancer or any number of conditions that doctors were unable to diagnose at the time. On March 1, Alcott went to visit her father on his deathbed. A stroke had made him an invalid, and his doctors did not think he would live much longer. The two shared a tender and tearful goodbye. Then Louisa headed home. She forgot to bundle up against the evening breeze and she came down with pneumonia. On March 4, Bronson Alcott died. In her fevered, unconscious state, Louisa never knew it. On March 6, at the age of fifty-five, Louisa May Alcott passed away.

BELOVED AUTHOR

People all over the world mourned the death of the woman they had come to know as "the Children's Friend." So much of *Little Women* had

Thousands mourned the loss of the great American writer Louisa May Alcott. She is best remembered for her books for young people.

been autobiographical. Alcott's readers felt as though they knew her, as if she were their own sister or friend. During her brief lifetime, she accomplished so much. Like the heroines of her stories, she made a difference in other people's lives. She used her talents to make the world a better place. Millions of copies of Alcott's books have been printed. Generations of girls have grown up reading *Little Women*, finding themselves in its pages. To this day, Louisa May Alcott remains one of the most beloved authors of all time.

Behind a Mask

During her lifetime, very few people knew that the beloved author of *Little Women* had also written countless murder mysteries and spine-tingling thrillers. Nearly all of Alcott's short stories were published under pen names, in part because of a gender bias. Readers in those days had preconceived ideas about the "sappy" types of stories women wrote, and most weren't interested in reading them. The use of a masculine pen name gave an author more credibility and increased her readership.

Recently, scholars began combing through Alcott's letters and diaries for clues to her secret identities. Once they discovered her pen names, they were able to trace hundreds of stories back to their true author. These works provide a fascinating glimpse into a very different part of Alcott's literary life. More than one hundred years after her death, collections of her stories have finally been published under the author's real name.

Timeline

1857 The Alcott family settles into Orchard House, which later becomes the setting of Alcott's best-selling novel *Little Women.*

1858 Alcott's beloved sister Lizzie dies after a bout with scarlet fever.

1860 Abraham Lincoln is elected president of the United States. Southern states begin to secede from the Union to form their own Confederacy.

1861 Confederates attack Fort Sumter in South Carolina, beginning the Civil War.

1862 Alcott travels to Washington, D.C., to nurse Union soldiers wounded in battle; she contracts typhoid and nearly dies.

1863 Alcott writes about her nursing experience in her widely acclaimed book *Hospital Sketches.*

President Lincoln issues the Emancipation Proclamation, freeing all slaves.

1865 Alcott travels to Europe as a companion to family friend and invalid, Anna Weld.

General Robert E. Lee and his Confederate troops surrender to Union General Ulysses S. Grant at Appomattox, ending the Civil War.

1867 Alcott accepts a position as editor of a children's magazine, *Merry's Museum.*

1868 Alcott draws on memories of her own childhood and family life to write her most popular and beloved children's novel, *Little Women.*

1870 Alcott publishes *An Old-Fashioned Girl;* she tours Europe with her youngest sister, May.

1871 From this point on, Alcott writes a new novel almost every year. Some of her best known works are *Little Men, Eight Cousins, Rose in Bloom,* and *Jo's Boys.*

1878 The Woman Suffrage Amendment is introduced in the United States Congress; it will not be ratified until 1920.

1879 Alcott becomes the first woman in Concord registered to vote in local school board elections. Sister May gives birth to Alcott's niece and namesake, Louisa May Nieriker ("Lulu").

1880 Following May's sudden and tragic death, Alcott adopts baby Lulu and raises her as her own daughter.

1888 Louisa May Alcott dies on March 6 at the age of fifty-five in Boston, Massachusetts.

To Find Out More

BOOKS

Chang, Ina. *Separate Battle: Women and the Civil War.* New York: Puffin Books, 1996.

Ford, Carin T. *Daring Women of the Civil War.* Berkeley Heights, NJ: Enslow Publishers, 2004.

Gormley, Beatrice. *Louisa May Alcott: Young Novelist.* New York: Simon & Schuster, 1999.

Graves, Kerry A. *The Girlhood Diary Of Louisa May Alcott, 1843–1846.* Mankato, MN: Capstone Press, 2000.

Meigs, Cornelia. *Invincible Louisa: The Story of the Author Of Little Women.* New York: Little, Brown & Company, 1995.

ORGANIZATIONS AND ONLINE SITES

Distinguished Women of Past and Present
http://www.distinguishedwomen.com/index.html

This lively site includes short biographies of famous women throughout history.

National Museum of Civil War Medicine
http://www.civilwarmed.org

Louisa May Alcott briefly served as a nurse during the Civil War and wrote about her experiences in *Hospital Sketches*. On this site, you can tour museum exhibits and access a special research library to learn more about the medical practices of the late 1800s.

Orchard House
http://www.louisamayalcott.org

Take a virtual tour of the Alcott family home where Louisa May Alcott wrote *Little Women*. This site includes detailed biographical information, special programs for teachers and students, and a collection of quotes entitled: "Alcott Wit and Wisdom."

A Note on Sources

Dozens of books have been written about Louisa May Alcott, beloved author of *Little Women*. The first was published by Ednah D. Cheney, a close personal friend of the Alcotts. Most contemporary books rely heavily on an extensive and definitive biography written by the world's leading Alcott scholar, Madeleine B. Stern. *Louisa May Alcott: A Biography* was first published in 1950. It was Stern who discovered the pseudonym that Alcott used when writing the sensational thrillers that helped her support her family in the early years of her career. With this information, Stern was able to identify hundreds of previously unrecognized stories and articles as the work of Alcott. Stern also worked to uncover the original, unedited versions of Alcott's diaries. Together, these sources provided a new and fascinating glimpse into the life and work of the author known as "the Children's Friend." Stern went on to edit numerous collections of Alcott's short stories, essays, letters, and journals. In 1996, with unprecedented access to a wealth of new material and years of additional research to draw from—Stern updated what remains the "standard" Alcott biography.

Other sources include *Louisa May: The World and Works of Louisa May Alcott* by Norma Johnston and *The Journals of Louisa May Alcott*, edited by Joel Myerson and Daniel Shealy. A number of general biographical works were consulted, as well as a few well-researched websites. Most notable: that of The Louisa May Alcott Memorial Association, which has turned Orchard House into a historic museum, wonderfully preserving the Alcott family legacy for generations to come.

—*Christin Ditchfield*

Index

About the Author

Christin Ditchfield is an author, conference speaker, and host of the nationally syndicated radio program, *Take It To Heart!* She has interviewed celebrity athletes such as gymnast Mary Lou Retton, NASCAR's Jeff Gordon, tennis pro Michael Chang, the NBA's David Robinson, and soccer great Michelle Akers. Her articles have been featured in magazines all over the world.

A former elementary school teacher, Ms. Ditchfield has written more than thirty books for children on a wide range of topics, including sports, science, and history. She recently wrote a young adult biography of Clara Barton for Franklin Watts. Ms. Ditchfield makes her home in Sarasota, Florida.